This book belongs to:

____

____

Books-In-Cursive

WILD FLOWER CHILDREN POEMS

Created by Angela M. Foster

Story by Elizabeth Gordon

Illustrated by Janet Laura Scott

ISBN-13: 978-1977908926
ISBN-10: 1977908926

INTRODUCTION

The ***Books-In-Cursive*** series publishes a variety of stories, poems, educational, etc. books in a cursive font. Why? There are so many "how to" and "practice" books out there for learning cursive handwriting, but what do you do after learning it? How do you keep the interest alive for many years to come? This is where the ***Books-In-Cursive*** series comes in. It fills the large void by providing books to read in cursive.

For more books of this series and others that are in cursive, "Like" the Facebook page called ***Cursive Reading Books*** at https://www.facebook.com/CursiveReadingBooks/

Hepatica

(Hepatica Triloba)

Hepatica comes bright and early,
Never tardy, never surly,
Wears a pretty lilac dress,
And gives out joy and happiness.

Innocence

(Houstonia Caerulea)

Innocence, the pretty thing,
Comes along in early Spring;
Wears sweet slips, the pretty pet,
In dainty shades of violet.

Shooting Star

(Dodecatheon Meadia)

Said Shooting Star, We're sure and steady,
And come as soon as we are ready;
We're not afraid of April's snows,
That's 'cause we're healthy, I suppose."

Pasque Flower

(Anemone Patens)

Pasque Flower is a prairie child,
Doesn't wait 'till days are mild,
But, wrapped in furs, she trips along,
Before the Robin sings his song.

Painted Trillium

(Trillium Undulatum)

Said Painted Trillium, "As you see,
Our folks observe the rule of three;
The styles may change, but still we
cling,
To our tri-cornered hats each spring."

Yellow Star Grass

(Hypoxis Hirsuta)

Yellow Star Grass hides in play,
Among the grasses every day;
But when you call "I spy," she's fair;
Then you can find her anywhere!

Solomon's Seal

(Polygonatum Biflorum)

Solomon's Seal said, looking wise,
"Each may do something if he tries;
I feed the honey bees, the dears,
And keep a record of my years!"

Marsh Marigold

(Caltha Palustris)

Marsh Marigold, bright cheerful thing,
Makes glad the days of early Spring;
She sprinkles gold stars one by one,
That look like bits chipped from the sun.

Pasture Rose

(Rosa Humilis)

Said Pasture Rose, "The Bumble bee,
Quite often leaves her babes with me;
I love to hold them next my heart;
I'm sorry when it's time to part!"

Day Flower

(Commelina Communis)

Day Flower wears a gown of blue,
That only lasts her one day through;
Her mother must be busy quite,
To make a new one every night.

Showy Lady's Slipper

(Cypripedium Hirsutum)

Showy Lady's Slipper knows,
She's the prettiest thing that grows;
Her Orchid Cousins in the city,
Say she's sweet as she is pretty.

Sweet White Violet

(Viola Pallens)

Sweet White Violet came to bring,
To us the fragrance of the Spring;
Dearest maid in all the wood,
Sweet and modest as she's good.

Red Clover

(Trifolium Pratense)

Red Clover swaying in the breeze,
Holds receptions for the bees;
Doesn't care for sweets himself,
But likes to feed each hungry elf.

Bunch Berry

(Cornus Canadensis)

Bunch Berry wears a gown of white,
And is a dainty woodland sprite;
She comes, the best of little mothers,
To bring her red-clothed Bunch Berry
brothers.

Jewelweed

(Impatiens Biflora)

"Beware of me," said Jewel Weed,
"I'm very dangerous, indeed;"
But still the fairies wouldn't stop,
They teased him just to hear him "pop."

Common Mallow

(Malva Rotundifolia)

Little Common Mallow said,
"I could not live inside a bed;
I like to roam just where I please;
The little children play I'm cheese!"

Rose Mallow

(Hibiscus Moscheutos)

Rose Mallow is a happy child,
She likes damp places, in the wild;
Blooms nearly all the summer through,
To make a lovely world for you.

Gold Thread

(Ceptis Trifolia)

Perhaps in woodland walks you've seen,
Sir Gold Thread dressed in evergreen;
They say the gnomes and fairies use,
His roots of gold to lace their shoes!

Monkey Flower

(Mimulus Ringens)

Young Monkey Flower put up a sign;
"Keep Out! This honey is all mine! "
But Bumble Bee just went ahead,
"I'm sure that don't mean me," he said.

Heal All

(Prunella Vulgaris)

Heal All wears a purple bonnet,
With some dainty colors on it;
Sometimes brightens her green clothes,
With tiny bits of purple bows.

Job's Tears or, Spiderwort

(Tradescantia Virginiana)

Job's Tears is such a funny lad!
He weeps all day! He isn't sad;
Just got the habit! All the season,
He weeps for neither rhyme nor reason.

Catnip

(Nepeta Cataria)

Old Dr. Catnip's glad to call,
On pussies big and pussies small;
But says, "If you'll all come to me,
I'll make you well without a fee."

St. John's Wort

(Hypericum Perforatum)

Common St. John's Wort is a tramp,
But he's a jolly little scamp;
Scatters his bloom along the way,
Like golden coins his way to pay.

Twin Flower

(Linnaea Borealis Americana)

Twin Flower Children, dainty pair,
Sprinkle fragrance on the air;
Seldom, elsewhere will you meet,
Flower Children half so sweet.

Bell Flower

(Campanula Rapunculoides)

Little Bell Flower ran away,
From the gardener one fine day,
Never did come back again;
Liked it better on the plain!

Star-Flower

(Trientalis Americana)

Dainty Star-Flower seemed to say,
As I raced through the woodland way;
"Don't be afraid, I'll give you light,
Just as the sky-stars do at night!"

Blue Spring Daisy

(Erigeron Pulchellas)

Blue Spring Daisy said, "I'm chilly,
In my lavender gown so frilly,
If I try to bloom too soon,
And so I wait till May or June."

Common Buttercup

(Ranunculus Acris)

Little Common Buttercup,
If you'll hold her gently up,
To your dimpled chin, will tell,
If you love butter very well.

False Lily Of The Valley

(Maianthemum Canadense)

False Lily of the Valley said,
"I'll choose another name instead;
Canada Mayflower it shall be;
There's nothing false, sir, about me."

Bellwort

(Uvularia Perfoliata)

If through the woods you'll walk in
May,
You'll see the Bellwort children play,
At hide and seek, in yellow coats,
With their wee cousins, sweet Wild Oats.

Downy Yellow Violet

(Viola Pubescens)

Downy Yellow Violet said,
"My woodland sister droops her head;
But I go romping on my way,
My face up turned to greet the day."

Queen Anne's Lace

(Daucus Carota)

The fairy babies simply race,
Each night to Madame Queen Anne's
Lace,
Cuddled so warmly to her breast,
She gives each babe a good night's rest.

Yellow Adder's Tongue

(Erythronium Americanum)

By dainty Yellow Adder's Tongue,
Such fairy elfin songs are sung,
That fairy folk come trooping out,
To hear what it is all about!

Rhododendron

(Rhododendron Maximum)

Rhododendron came to town,
In her green and rose pink gown;
She's so pretty that we give,
Her the nicest spots to live.

Lamb-Kill

(Kalmia Augustifolia)

Lamb-Kill's as pretty as can be;
He can't be trusted though, you see,
He's mischievous, and feeds the sheep,
Some sort of stuff that makes them
sleep.

Canada Lily

(Lilium Canadense)

Canada Lily grows quite wild,
But she's a gentle graceful child,
She loves the meadows where she plays,
Happily through the summer days.

Cream-Cup

(Platystemon Californica)

Cream-Cup comes, the pretty thing,
To gladden California's Spring,
You'll meet them everywhere in flocks,
Clambering over hills and rocks.

Baby Blue Eyes

(Nemophila Insignis)

Baby Blue Eyes comes in Spring,
Dainty dimpled smiling thing;
Calls to us from far away,
Won't you please come out to play?"

California Larkspur

(Delphinium Americanum)

California Larkspur plays,
With Golden Poppies all his days,
Prettiest children ever seen,
Dressed in gold and blue and green.

Wild Morning Glory

(Convolulus Sepium)

Wild Morning Glory runs away,
Along the woodland paths to play;
She climbs about with easy grace,
And hangs her bright bells every place.

Cardinal Flower

(Lobelia Cardinalis)

Stately Madame Cardinal Flower,
Holds receptions by the hour;
Invites those whom she likes the best,
And Humming Bird's her favorite guest.

Turks Cap Lily

(Lilium Superbum)

Said Turks Cap Lily, "As you see,
I'm as industrious as can be;
That's why I'm rich, and can afford,
To give such swarms of bees their board."

Wild Columbine

(Aquilegia Canadensis)

"I keep my sweets," said Columbine,
"For Humming Bird, a friend of mine;
He comes at sun-down every night,
And is so grateful and polite."

White Clover

(Trifolium Repens)

The Robin heard white Clover say,
"When I'm grown I'll be Sweet Hay,
To feed the cow so she can give,
Nice milk to help wee children live."

Evening Primrose

(Onogra Biennis)

Said Evening Primrose, "I wake up,
When twilight comes, and fill my cup,
With sweetest honey for my friends,
The moths, who come when day-time
ends."

Wild Geranium or Cranesbill

(Geranium Maculatum)

Along the wooded roads I grow,
And children pluck me as they go,
And say my flowers are sweet and gay,
Which makes me happy all the day.

Fireweed

(Epilobium Augustifolium)

When fire fiends through the woodland race,
Leaving a blackened barren place,
Then Fire Weed knows that it's his duty,
To make the burned land bloom with beauty.

Lupine

(Lupinus Perrenis)

In sand dunes hot or meadows gay,
The little Lupines love to play;
In dainty gowns of violet blue,
They'll nod a glad "Good-day" to you.

Dutchman's Breeches

(Dicentra Cucullaria)

The daintiest twins in all the land,
Dutchman's Breeches, hand in hand,
In Springtime tumble down the hill,
Just like another Jack and Jill.

Skunk Cabbage

(Symplocarpus Foetidus)

Skunk Cabbage is a handsome thing,
Comes while it is cold in Spring;
Protects his babes from wind and storm,
In a big coat that keeps them warm.

Jack In The Pulpit

(Arisaema Triphyllum)

Each Sunday, on a mossy mound,
The Flower Children gather round,
Jack-In-The-Pulpit, while he teaches,
Each one, to practice what he preaches.

Blue Flag

(Iris Versicolor)

Blue Flag's as pretty as can be;
Cousin to Mam'selle Fleur De Lis;
Loves cool damp places, and is fond,
Of living near a stream or pond.

Pearly Everlasting

(Anaphalis Margaritacea)

Around the hillsides in the sun,
The Pearly Everlastings run;
Never find enough to eat,
But still they're plump and clean and
neat.

Water Lily

(Castalia Adorato)

Water Lily is a queen,
Wears sweet robes of white and green;
Sleeps so sweetly all night long,
Lulled by Green Frog's slumber song.

Yellow Pond Lily

(Nymphaea Advena)

Yellow Pond Lily laughed and said,
"Some one splashed water on my head;"
Said Spotted Trout, "Perhaps t'was I,
When I jumped out to catch a fly."

Water Arum

(Calla Palustris)

Water Arum shares his bog,
With his good neighbor Mr. Frog;
Dressed in his best, when day time
ends,
The Frog's grand concert he attends.

Skull Cap

(Scutellaria Integrifolia)

Skull Cap keeps a hat shop; he,
Is just as busy as can be;
That's where the fairies, cunning chaps,
Get all their pointed tasseled caps.

Bull Thistle

(Cirsium Lanceolatum)

Bull Thistle waves a thousand lances,
So bugs and beetles take no chances;
But butterflies and honey bees,
Are welcome any time they please.

Common Mullein

(Verbascum Thapsus)

Common Mullein's lots of fun,
He loves the children every one;
His velvet leaves when torn he'll lend,
To any fairy who will mend.

Broad Leaved Arrow Head

(Sagittaria Latifolia)

Lovely Broad Leaved Arrow Head,
Lives in Madame River's bed;
Loves to wade and splash all day,
And with the Minnow children play.

Large Purple Orchis

(Habenaria Fimbriata)

Large Purple Orchis loves to grow,
Where crowds of people do not go;
But you're quite welcome, if you'll
tramp,
To where she lives (It's rather damp).

Butter And Eggs

(Linaria Vulgaris)

Said Butter and Eggs, "We can afford,
To give Sir Bumble Bee his board;
But when he's gone we close the door,
Or we'd have Ants in by the score!"

Indian Paint Brush

(Castilleja Coccinea)

Indian Paint Brush holds his cup,
Of brilliant scarlet petals up;
That's all he does; for he's a shirk,
And lives on other people's work.

Black Eyed Susan

(Rudbeckia Hirta)

Saucy Little Black-Eyed Susan,
When her mother caught her snoozin',
Rubbed her sleepy eyes and said,
"Guess I'll toddle off to bed."

Moss Pink

(Phlox Subulata)

Little Moss Pink creeps around,
All summer on the sandy ground;
Daintiest creature ever seen,
In her gown of pink and green.

Cat-Tail

(Typha Latifolia)

The Cat-Tail people roam around,
Through any sort of marshy ground;
If you'll go by their house at night,
You'll see their yellow candle light.

Common Plantain

(Plantago Major)

Common Plantain thought he'd play,
Around the house one summer day;
Gardener called him "Naughty Weed!"
Which made him very sad indeed!

Common Milk Weed

(Asclepias Syrica)

Said Common Milk Weed, When I've
fed,
The bees, I put my babes to bed,
In silken cradles, where they sway,
Rocked by the little Winds all day.

Lady's Sorrel

(Oxalis Cornucalate)

Lady's Sorrel sleeps so tight,
Throughout the peaceful summer night;
But her eyes fly open wide,
When Sunbeam frolics by her side!

Downy Phlox

(Phlox Pilosa)

Said Downy Phlox, "Of all the West,
I love the rolling prairies best;"
Cousin Sweet William smiled and said,
"I like my own soft garden bed."

Showy Golden Rod

(Solidago Speciosa)

"Our family is so large you see,"
Said Showy Golden Rod to me,
"It keeps me nodding all the day,
To cousins who go by this way!"

New England Aster

(Aster Nova-Anglae)

New England Aster said, "Dear me!
I've been as lazy as can be;"
So dressed in purple, off she flew,
And traveled all the country through.

Smooth Aster

(Aster Laevis)

Wild Smooth Aster loves to play,
Along the roadside every day;
Waving her banner blue in glee,
Perhaps to you, perhaps to me.

Downy Gentian

(Gentiana Puberula)

Downy Gentian rings his bell,
His friends the butterflies to tell,
It's honey time; and how they all,
Come trooping when they hear his call.

Closed Gentian

(Gentiana Andrewsii)

"O Bottle Gentian," begged the bees,
"Open and give us honey, please?"
But Bottle Gentian shook his head,
"Belongs to Bumble Bee," he said.

Heart Leaved Aster

(Aster Cordifolius)

"I wear my heart outside, you know,"
Said Heart Leaved Aster, "That is so,
The bird, the Butterfly, the bee,
May tell their secrets all to me."

Silver Rod

(Solidago Bicolor)

Said Silver Rod, "My cousins all,
Wear robes of gold the livelong Fall;
It's unbecoming to me quite,
And so I dress in creamy white."

Virgin's Bower

(Clematis Verticillaris)

Said Virgin's Bower, "I spend my time,
Teaching the younger ones to climb;
But when Fall comes we all look weird,
For then folks call us, 'Old Man's
Beard.'"

Ground Ivy

(Nepeta Hederacea)

Ground Ivy, "Gill-Run-Over-The-Ground,"
Scatters her purple flowers around;
She says she dearly loves to stay,
Where little children romp and play.

Clintonia

(Clintonia Borealis)

Clintonia borrowed with a smile,
Cousin Lily-Of-The-Valley's style;
The gown became her very well,
Trimmed with her own sweet yellow
bell.

Frostweed

(Helianthemum Canadense)

Frostweed's sometimes called Rock Rose,
He doesn't mind how cold it grows;
Laughs, and thinks it's rather nice,
To trim his cap with bits of ice.